WINTER OLYMPICS

ALL-TIME GREATS

BY ANTHONY STREETER

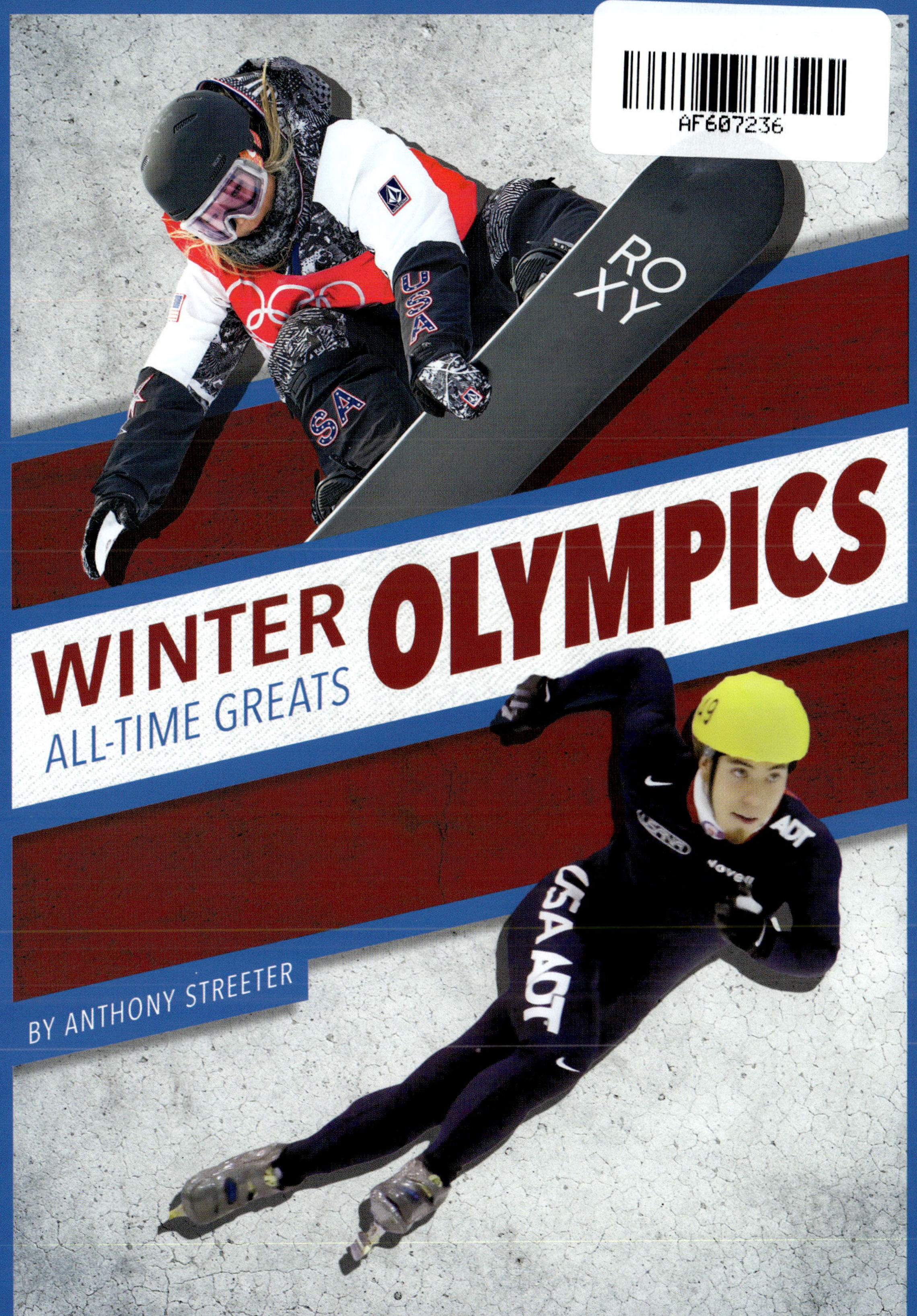

Book design by Jake Slavik
Cover design by Jake Slavik

Photographs ©: Ulrik Pedersen/Cal Sport Media/ZUMA Press/AP Images, cover (top), 1 (top); Douglas C. Pizac/AP Images, cover (bottom), 1 (bottom); Bettmann/Getty Images, 4, 7; Bruce Bennett/Getty Images Studios/Getty Images, 8; Simon Bruty/Hulton Archive/Getty Images, 10; Alexander Hassenstein/Bongarts/Getty Images, 13; Matthew Stockman/Getty Images Sport/ Getty Images, 15; Alex Livesey/Getty Images Sport/Getty Images, 16; Sampics/Corbis Sport/ Getty Images, 18; Maddie Meyer/Getty Images Sport/Getty Images, 20

Press Box Books, an imprint of Press Room Editions.

ISBN
978-1-63494-866-1 (library bound)
978-1-63494-884-5 (paperback)
978-1-63494-919-4 (epub)
978-1-63494-902-6 (hosted ebook)

Library of Congress Control Number: 2023923060

Distributed by North Star Editions, Inc.
2297 Waters Drive
Mendota Heights, MN 55120
www.northstareditions.com

Printed in the United States of America
082024

ABOUT THE AUTHOR

Anthony Streeter is a former sportswriter who has written for various newspapers. He lives in Columbia, Missouri, with his wife and three kids.

TABLE OF CONTENTS

HENIE

CHAPTER 1
WINTER WONDERS

The modern Olympic Games began in 1896. Some early Olympics included figure skating events. However, it wasn't until 1924 that the first Olympic Winter Games were held. That year, 11-year-old **Sonja Henie** finished eighth in women's figure skating. Before long she became the sport's biggest star. The Norwegian won the next three Olympic gold medals. Fans were drawn to her graceful style. Later she became a star in Hollywood.

A new era in figure skating began in 1948. **Dick Button** won gold by performing jumps never seen in the sport. Those moves helped the American win a second gold medal in 1952.

BIRGER RUUD

Birger Ruud won a gold medal in men's large hill ski jumping in 1936. It was his second gold in a row. Ruud might have won more medals. However, the next two Winter Games were canceled due to World War II (1939–45). After the war, Ruud won another ski jumping silver medal in 1948.

Germany is a dominant country in the sliding sports. Bobsledder **Andreas Ostler** helped start that tradition. Competing for West Germany, Ostler drove both two-man and four-man sleds to victory in 1952. No bobsledder had done that before.

Toni Sailer grew up skiing in the Austrian Alps. No type of racing was too difficult for him.

10 NOR 6
FRA
1321
USA
34
135

He displayed his skills at the 1956 Winter Games. Sailer won all three men's alpine events. None of the races were close.

The Soviet Union won six of seven gold medals in men's hockey from 1964 to 1988. Goalie **Vladislav Tretiak** helped win three of them. No man has more hockey gold medals. However, the Soviet coach benched him during a medal-round game in 1980. The United States came into that game as huge underdogs.

But American goalie **Jim Craig** had the performance of his life. Then team captain **Mike Eruzione** scored the game-winning goal. The win is known as the "Miracle on Ice." Team USA went on to win the gold medal.

However, the most dominant performance at those 1980 Olympics came on a different sheet of ice. Over nine days, American speed skater **Eric Heiden** won all five men's gold medals in that sport. The races ranged from 500 to 10,000 meters. Heiden set Olympic records in all five. He also set a world record in the 10,000-meter race.

STAT SPOTLIGHT

WINTER OLYMPIC RECORD

MOST INDIVIDUAL GOLD MEDALS IN A SINGLE OLYMPICS

Eric Heiden: 5 (1980)

BLAIR
MIZUNO
USA

CHAPTER 2
GOLD-MEDAL GREATS

Since Sonja Henie, no woman had defended her Olympic figure skating gold medal. **Katarina Witt** finally changed that. The East German star drew in audiences with her elegant skating. In both 1984 and 1988, Witt faced tough competition. Yet each time she proved to be the best.

A large cheering section always seemed to follow **Bonnie Blair**. The American speed skater gave her fans plenty to celebrate. Blair broke out at the 1988 Winter Games, earning a gold and a bronze medal. She also set the world record in the 500-meter race. Her long strides helped her break away from other skaters. Blair raced to four more gold medals at the 1992 and 1994 Olympics.

No country has as many Winter Olympic medals as Norway. And three Norwegians combined to win dozens of them. **Bjørn Dæhlie** competed in the 1992, 1994, and 1998 Olympics as a cross-country skier. Eight of his 12 medals were golds. Biathlete **Ole Einar Bjørndalen** won his eighth gold in his sixth and final Olympics in 2014. He retired

STAT SPOTLIGHT

WINTER OLYMPIC RECORD

CAREER MEDALS BY AN AMERICAN WOMAN

Bonnie Blair: 6

with 13 total medals. However, nobody won more medals than **Marit Bjørgen**. The cross-country skier won 15 medals over five Olympics. That included five medals at both the 2010 and 2018 Games. Bjørgen also tied her countrymen with eight golds.

For many years, **Janica Kostelić** had an exhausting training routine. All of her hard work set her up for success at the 2002 Olympics. The Croatian alpine skier won three gold medals plus a silver. That performance made her the first woman to win three alpine golds in one Olympics. She also became the first alpine skier to win four medals at a single Olympics.

The first things most fans noticed about **Apolo Anton Ohno** were his goatee and bandana. Fans couldn't ignore his racing

STAR FROM DOWN UNDER

While growing up in Australia, Alisa Camplin was a skilled sailor and gymnast. It wasn't until her teenage years that she tried aerial skiing. In 2002, she won the Olympic title. She became the first Australian woman to win gold at the Winter Games. And Camplin earned it on two broken ankles. Four years later, she won a bronze medal.

skills, though. Ohno weaved in and out of his short-track speed skating competitors. And he usually beat them. Ohno retired after the 2010 Olympics. No American has won more than his eight Winter Olympic medals.

NORBERG
Kämpela
SWEDEN

CHAPTER 3
NEXT-LEVEL STARS

People in the Netherlands began ice skating hundreds of years ago. Many of the fastest speed skaters still come from the small European country. **Ireen Wüst** dominated the sport like no one else. She won 13 medals in long-track speed skating from 2006 to 2022. That is four better than the next best speed skater. Wüst's six gold medals are tied for the most in her sport.

Curling became an Olympic sport in 1998. **Anette Norberg** led Sweden to the women's gold medal in both 2006 and 2010. No other women's curling team has won twice in a row.

Shaun White was easy to spot in 2006 because of his floppy red hair. His high-flying snowboarding skills helped, too. The US teen won gold in the men's halfpipe. In 2010, his first run was so good no one could match it. His second run was just a victory lap. And White wanted it to be special. He ended it with an amazing trick called the Double McTwist 1260. In five Olympics, White won three golds. No snowboarder has won more.

South Koreans had big dreams for **Yuna Kim** in 2010. The figure skater delivered with a nearly flawless performance. Kim's score shattered her own world record. South Korea had never won a Winter Olympic medal in a sport other than speed skating. Kim changed that with a gold in figure skating.

Team USA beat Canada in 1998 to win the first Olympic gold medal in women's hockey. Then Canada won the next four.

ESTER LEDECKA

Ester Ledecka entered the 2018 Olympics as a favorite in snowboard racing. She stunned fans by winning the alpine skiing super-G instead. It was one of the biggest upsets in Olympic history. Then she won gold in parallel giant slalom snowboarding. The Czech star became the first athlete to win gold medals in two sports in one Olympics.

Canadian **Marie-Philip Poulin** scored the winning goals in 2010 and 2014. After settling for silver in 2018, Canada won another gold in 2022. Once again, Poulin scored the winning goal. "Captain Clutch" became the first player to score a goal in four gold-medal games.

Chloe Kim was just 17 years old at the 2018 Olympics. The US snowboarder made history in the halfpipe. She became the first woman to land back-to-back 1080 spins. Those tricks earned her a near-perfect score and a gold medal. Four years later, Kim easily defended her gold.

A new teen took center stage at the 2022 Olympics. China's **Eileen Gu** won gold medals in the skiing halfpipe and big air events. Gu also won a silver medal in slopestyle. She became the first freestyle skier to win three medals in one Olympics.

STAT SPOTLIGHT

OLYMPIC RECORD

WOMEN'S HALFPIPE SNOWBOARDING SCORE

98.25 / 100: Chloe Kim (2018)

TIMELINE

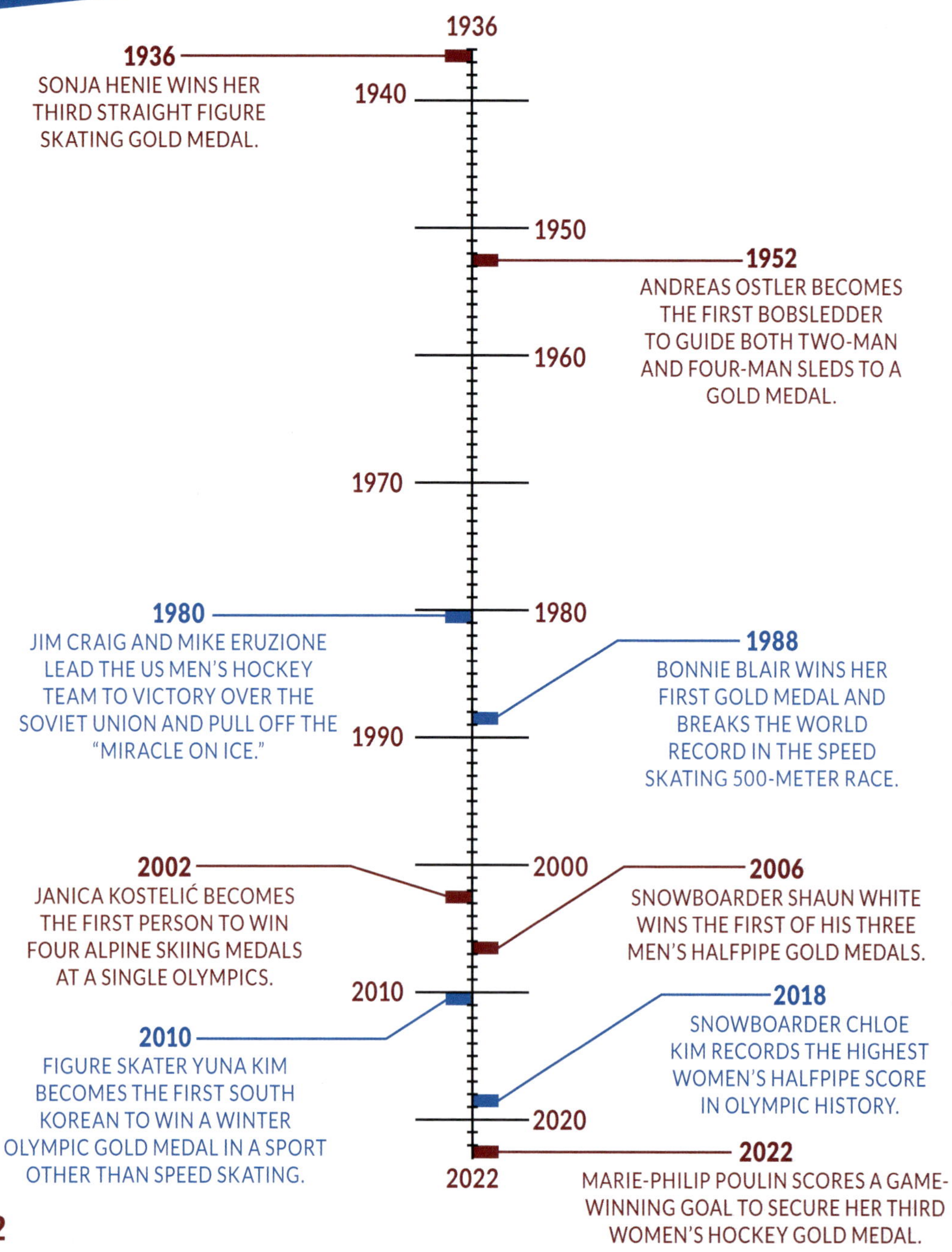
1936
1940
1950
1960
1970
1980
1990
2000
2010
2020
2022
1936
SONJA HENIE WINS HER THIRD STRAIGHT FIGURE SKATING GOLD MEDAL.
1952
ANDREAS OSTLER BECOMES THE FIRST BOBSLEDDER TO GUIDE BOTH TWO-MAN AND FOUR-MAN SLEDS TO A GOLD MEDAL.
1980
JIM CRAIG AND MIKE ERUZIONE LEAD THE US MEN'S HOCKEY TEAM TO VICTORY OVER THE SOVIET UNION AND PULL OFF THE "MIRACLE ON ICE."
1988
BONNIE BLAIR WINS HER FIRST GOLD MEDAL AND BREAKS THE WORLD RECORD IN THE SPEED SKATING 500-METER RACE.
2002
JANICA KOSTELIĆ BECOMES THE FIRST PERSON TO WIN FOUR ALPINE SKIING MEDALS AT A SINGLE OLYMPICS.
2006
SNOWBOARDER SHAUN WHITE WINS THE FIRST OF HIS THREE MEN'S HALFPIPE GOLD MEDALS.
2010
FIGURE SKATER YUNA KIM BECOMES THE FIRST SOUTH KOREAN TO WIN A WINTER OLYMPIC GOLD MEDAL IN A SPORT OTHER THAN SPEED SKATING.
2018
SNOWBOARDER CHLOE KIM RECORDS THE HIGHEST WOMEN'S HALFPIPE SCORE IN OLYMPIC HISTORY.
2022
MARIE-PHILIP POULIN SCORES A GAME-WINNING GOAL TO SECURE HER THIRD WOMEN'S HOCKEY GOLD MEDAL.

CHAMPIONSHIP FACTS

WINTER OLYMPICS

First held: 1924

Most Winter Olympic medals: Marit Bjørgen, 15

Most Winter Olympic gold medals: Marit Bjørgen, Ole Einar Bjørndalen, and Bjørn Dæhlie, 8

Most Winter Olympic medals by country: Norway, 405

Stats are accurate through 2023.

MORE INFORMATION

To learn more about the Winter Olympics, go to **pressboxbooks.com/AllAccess**.

These links are routinely monitored and updated to provide the most current information available.

GLOSSARY

captain
A player who serves as the leader of a team.

era
A period of time in history.

freestyle
Events in which the focus is on showmanship and tricks, rather than racing.

modern
Relating to the recent past.

retired
Stopped competing.

sliding sports
Olympic sports that involve racing down an icy track. Bobsled, luge, and skeleton are Olympic sliding sports.

tradition
A way of doing something that is passed down over many years.

underdogs
Individuals or teams that are not expected to win.

upsets
Unexpected victories by supposedly weaker individuals or teams.

INDEX